Travel & Tourism

Careers for Today
Travel & Tourism

Marjorie Rittenberg Schulz

Franklin Watts

New York • London • Toronto • Sydney

Developed by: 𝛺 **Visual Education Corporation
Princeton, NJ**

Cover Photograph: Joyce Photographics/Photo Researchers, Inc.

Photo Credits: p. 2 Joyce Photographics/Photo Researchers, Inc.; p.6 Peter Russell Clemens/International Stock Photography; p. 12 Princess Cruises; p. 14 Robert Bruschini/Hyatt Regency, Princeton; p. 20 American Airlines; p. 26 Robert Bruschini/Love to Travel; p.32 Robert Bruschini/A-1 Limousine Service; p. 35 Tom & Michele Grimm/International Stock Photography; p. 38 G.E. Pakenham/ International Stock Photography; p. 44 Robert Bruschini/A-1 Limousine Service; p. 50 Marriott Corporation; p. 53 David Madison/ Bruce Coleman, Inc.; p. 56 Robert Bruschini/Studio B; p. 59 Robert Bruschini/Studio B; p. 62 Meeting Planners International; p. 68 United States Census Bureau; p. 74 Princess Cruises; p. 76 Pat Canova/Bruce Coleman, Inc.; p. 78 Princess Cruises; p. 80 Peter Russell Clemens/International Stock Photography

Library of Congress Cataloging-in-Publication Data

Schulz, Marjorie Rittenberg
Travel and tourism/Marjorie Rittenberg Schulz.
p.   cm. — (Careers for today)
Includes bibliographical references (p.   ).
Summary: Describes the various careers available in tourism and provides suggestions for students interested in obtaining such work.
ISBN 0-531-10975-5
1. Tourist trade — Vocational guidance — Juvenile literature. [1. Tourist trade — Vocational guidance. 2. Vocational guidance.] I. Title II. Series: Schulz, Marjorie Rittenberg. Careers for today.
G155.5.S38   1990
338.4'79102373 — dc20   90-12235 CIP AC

Contents

Introduction   7
1. Bellhop and Doorkeeper   15
2. Airline Reservations Agent   21
3. Travel Agent   27
4. Limousine Driver and Tour-Bus Driver   33
5. Tour Guide   39
6. Taxi Dispatcher   45
7. Caterer   51
8. Truck-Stop Operator   57
9. Convention Planner   63
10. Bookkeeper, Secretary, and Clerk   69
11. Cruise Director   75
12. Getting the Job: Tips for the Reader   81
Sources   95
Index   96

Introduction

Beth and Steve have been saving for two years to take a trip. They know that they want to go someplace warm and sunny, but they do not know where to begin. Whom do they call?

Mike wants to have a dinner party for his parents' twenty-fifth wedding anniversary. He needs someone to help plan and prepare the food for thirty guests. Whom does he call?

Beth, Steve, and Mike have simple problems that can be solved with phone calls to workers in the travel and tourism field. Beth and Steve will call a travel agent to give them information on vacations and to help them decide on a place to go. The agent will advise them about what they can do within their price range. Then the agent will make all the arrangements for their air travel and hotel room. Mike will call a caterer to take care of the food for his parents' party.

Workers in travel and tourism help visitors to new cities by running tours. They help business and leisure travelers arrange airplane flights and taxi or limousine service. They also address the needs of truck drivers for quality food and other services.

This book can help young readers see the many opportunities open to them in the booming field of travel and tourism.

Travel and Tourism Today

When most Americans thought of travel fifty years ago, they thought of driving the family car to the place they wanted to visit. Life moved at a slower pace, and travel was often slower, too. Travel and tourism have come a long way since then. Now we can travel thousands of miles in a few hours. And when we arrive, we look to the services provided by trained professionals to make our stay as enjoyable as possible.

More people are traveling today, for leisure and business, than ever before. They are taking long weekends and short trips, traveling over holiday breaks, and booking convention stays. They want transportation, food service, and entertainment to make their trips relaxing and memorable.

This increase in demand means millions of job opportunities at many different levels. Some positions call for training on the job. Others require that applicants have some training or special skills before they can be hired. Many of the jobs offer the chance to advance.

The travel and tourism field includes jobs in transportation, tourism, and food service. These jobs are related to those in the hospitality and recreation field. Among the jobs in this field are those you will read about in this book: bellhop and doorkeeper, airline reservations agent, travel agent, limousine driver or tour-bus driver, tour guide, taxi dispatcher, caterer, truck-stop operator, convention planner, bookkeeper, secretary, clerk, and cruise director. The field includes many other jobs, of course, but these provide a good sampling of the range of skills required.

Work in travel and tourism is aimed at providing service to people. Even so, technology and the use of machines play an important part in travel and tourism today. Using computerized reservation systems, travel agents can more quickly help customers book airplane flights. These systems help agents scan information on thousands of airline flights. The systems tell the agents the origin and destination cities, dates, times of departure and arrival, fares, and availability. Agents can also use the systems to check on the availability of hotel rooms, rental cars, train reservations, and package tours. All this work can be done in seconds, while the client waits to make a decision. And once the client has decided, the agent can book the flight, room, rental car, train, or tour in seconds.

The face of travel and tourism is changing today. But jobs in this field still require the same hard work, training, and skills that they did in the past. Careers in travel and tourism can be as inviting as a sunset viewed from the deck of a cruise ship, as rewarding as the success of an independent agent, and as satisfying as the smile on the face of a happy client.

Many workers in travel and tourism share a special benefit of their careers. They enjoy the pleasure of visiting new places and seeing new sights. Travel agents receive lower prices on their own travel. They can also join in special trips to new resorts. These trips are arranged to introduce them to a resort or hotel so that they can sell it better to their clients. Tour guides have the pleasant task of showing people around the great natural, historical, and cultural treasures of the world.

Outlook for the Future

Employment in travel and tourism has grown rapidly in the past decades. This growth is expected to continue in the future. In the mid-1980s, one in every eight new jobs was related to the travel and tourism field. The chart below tracks the growth of jobs in three segments of this industry: airlines, amusement parks, and hotels and other lodging places.

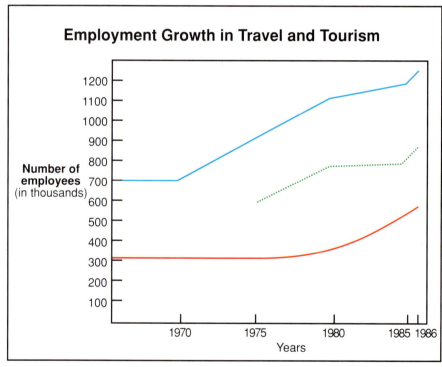

Employment Growth in Travel and Tourism

Number of employees (in thousands)

Years

Key:

Airlines

Amusement parks

Hotels and other lodging places

(Statistics NA before 1975)

Source: U.S Bureau of Labor Statistics.

10

The strength of the U.S. economy has a strong effect on travel and tourism. When the economy is strong, people spend more on travel, and employment is up. When the economy is weak, people and businesses cut back on travel. That may mean that jobs are cut back, too.

But the future looks bright for travel and tourism. Travel agents are one example. Today more than 100,000 people work as travel agents in the United States. That number is expected to grow to nearly 300,000 by the year 2000.

Travel

In 1989 alone, Americans took more than 1.3 billion trips. Sixty-nine percent of that travel was for pleasure; 24 percent was for business or conventions. The airlines carried over 457 million passengers in that year. Cruise business has increased, too. The number of cruise passengers grew 10 percent in that year. Many of those American travelers went to other countries, but most travel was domestic, or within the United States.

Many travelers come to the United States from other lands. Over 42 million people from other countries are expected to visit the United States in 1990. The British, French, Japanese, and West Germans are the most frequent foreign travelers to the United States. This foreign travel is important to the job market, too. Every 52 foreign visitors to this country means another job is created.

To encourage even more travel, airlines will probably be adding more executive or business-class sections on airplanes. They will also ex-

Cruises, which often include educational and recreational programs, are becoming increasingly popular.

pand their frequent-flyer programs. These plans allow travelers who fly many trips to earn credits for free trips or reduced fares. Another way to increase travel is to offer package deals. These plans combine airline, hotel, and other travel arrangements. These packages attract travelers, who pay just one price for all their travel needs.

Package educational and vacation tours are on the rise. This growth is a good trend for tour guides, tour-bus and limousine drivers, and airline reservations and travel agents.

Vacation cruises are becoming more popular. Many cruises are geared toward special groups. These include senior citizens, families, couples, or singles. Cruises are still underbooked, however. This has kept prices down and availability up. If bookings increase, there will be a greater demand for workers by cruise companies.

Food Service

Food service is one of the fastest-growing industries in the United States today. Travel- and tourism-related food workers will be in high demand as we move through the 1990s. Hotel and motel food services will profit from the expected rise in business and leisure travel.

Hotels and convention centers will gain from the growth in the number of conventions. Almost 600,000 conventions and meetings took place in a recent year. Cities are planning new convention centers. They promote their advantages to business and professional groups in the hopes of getting more of this convention business. Conventions require the efforts of many workers. The convention planner, described in this book, is key to a successful meeting.

Caterers will also gain from the growing demand for food service. Caterers prepare and serve food for home dinner parties, luncheons, weddings, and other celebrations. Large catering companies will be increasingly called on to provide good food at conventions and meetings that attract people from out of town. They are likely to see increased demand from institutions and businesses in their own area as well.

Truck-stop operators will be busier in the coming years as well. Nearly 2.5 million truck drivers carry one-quarter of the nation's freight each year, and the demand for trucking is expected to grow by 20 percent by the year 2000. With more truckers on the road, more truck stops will be built, and existing stops will be expanded. This will make more jobs for the people who serve food and otherwise help truckers as they rest on their trips.

Chapter 1
Bellhop and Doorkeeper

There are many people guests see when they arrive at a hotel. The doorkeeper helps them out of their taxis or arranges for their cars to be parked. The doorkeeper then shows the guests inside the hotel.

Once inside, the guests are greeted by the desk clerk, who checks on the reservations. When the room arrangements are complete, the keys are handed to the bellhop. The bellhop shows guests to the elevator and up to their rooms.

Bellhop

Bellhops got their name 200 years ago. When travelers came to the door of an inn, the bellhop rang a bell to signal that guests had arrived.

Education, Training, and Salary   Many hotels prefer to hire someone with a high school education. Other hotels may not require it.

Bellhops are trained on the job. In smaller hotels, they may begin working as bellhops. But at larger hotels, they may start out as elevator operators or in other service jobs.

The average salary for bellhops is $4.00 to $6.00 an hour, plus tips. Bellhops earn more in larger hotels because there are more guests, which means more tips. Bellhops usually receive free meals at work. They may also get benefits like medical insurance and paid vacations. The hotel also gives them uniforms to wear while working.

Job Description   Bellhops carry guests' luggage to their rooms, unlock the door, and help them get settled. Bellhops may put bags on a luggage rack. They may also hang up coats or other clothing.

Bellhops are also responsible for making sure that the heat or air conditioning in the room is set at a comfortable temperature. They check to see that lights and the television are working. They show guests how to use pay television. And they tell guests whom to call for more information. They also explain about room service or valet service and how to obtain those services.

Often guests ask bellhops about what restaurants are nearby. Bellhops who can answer these questions help guests feel at home.

In larger hotels, guests may ask bellhops to run errands, such as going to a nearby store or mailing letters or packages. Bellhops often receive tips for performing these jobs.

Bellhops do a lot of physical work. They lift suitcases and baggage in and out of cars and bring them into the hotel. They carry the bags themselves or use carts to move the bags. Bellhops spend most of each day on their feet.

Some hotels also employ porters. They handle baggage, like bellhops, but generally work outside the hotel. They are sometimes in charge of arranging for bags to be shipped to other areas. They may also lift furniture, convention displays, or other items that need to be moved.

Bellhops and porters generally work in eight-hour shifts. Because hotels are open all night, a shift is on duty at all times. Shifts are changed so that all bellhops and porters work some weekends or evenings.

16

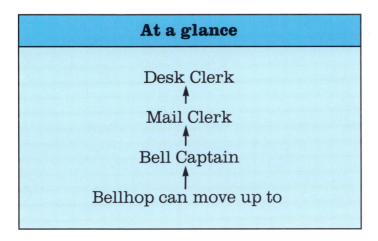

At a glance

Desk Clerk
↑
Mail Clerk
↑
Bell Captain
↑
Bellhop can move up to

Outlook for Jobs   With hard work and a high school education, a bellhop might be promoted to be bell captain. Bell captains usually work in medium-sized or large hotels. They are in charge of training and supervising the bellhops.

The captain sets work schedules for the bellhops and gives them their assignments. The bell captain is also responsible for keeping track of the hours that bellhops work. Captains make sure that bellhops are paid the right amount.

Sometimes guests have problems or complaints about their luggage. The bell captain must handle these problems politely and efficiently.

With much experience and good work records, bellhops may work their way up to be mail clerks, room clerks, or desk clerks.

More motels and economy inns are being built today. At most motels, guests carry their own luggage to and from their rooms. So motels do not hire bellhops. But as hotel business grows, more hotels will be built. Then more jobs will open up for bellhops in the future.

17

Doorkeeper

Education, Training, and Salary
There is no education requirement for doorkeepers.

New doorkeepers are trained on the job by experienced doorkeepers. They may work at other jobs in the hotel first, such as bellhop.

Doorkeepers usually start at about $4.00 an hour plus tips. With experience, they may earn up to $15,000 a year. Union members earn more than nonunion members. Doorkeepers usually get benefits like paid vacations, sick leave, medical insurance, and retirement pay.

Job Description
The doorkeeper is the first person a guest meets on arriving at some apartment buildings and hotels.

At a hotel, doorkeepers help guests out of taxis. Or they might arrange to have the guests' cars parked at the hotel garage. When a guest leaves the hotel, doorkeepers may hail a taxi. Or they call the parking garage for the guest's car.

Many people staying at hotels are business travelers and vacationers from out of town. So giving directions to places of interest or suggesting a restaurant may be part of the hotel doorkeeper's job. The doorkeeper helps guests with information or services that they need. The more friendly and courteous the service the doorkeeper provides, the more likely the guest is to give a tip.

Some doorkeepers work in large apartment buildings in major cities. They assist the people who live there and those who visit the residents. When a guest arrives, the doorkeeper phones the resident. Doorkeepers at apartments also hail taxis or call for cars parked in the garage.

18

Apartment doorkeepers often handle all packages delivered to the building. They may accept packages for tenants. Or they may direct delivery people to the service entrance or the loading dock.

Doorkeepers at hotels and apartments also act as security workers. Since they stand at the entrances, they see all people who come up to the door. They watch for people who look suspicious. They must be alert to people who might cause trouble. If they see anything wrong, they call the management or the police.

Rain or snow, 10 degrees below zero or 100 degrees above, doorkeepers stand at their posts outside the building. They may stand for hours at a time, but still they must be cheerful and polite to tenants and guests.

Outlook for Jobs   Since few hotels and apartments employ doorkeepers, job possibilities are few. Doorkeepers seem to keep the jobs they have, so turnover is low. A few openings come up as doorkeepers retire.

For more information on bellhops and doorkeepers, write to:

American Hotel and Motel Association
1201 New York Avenue, NW
Washington, DC 20005
(202) 289–3100

Hotel Employees and Restaurant Employees
   International Union
1219 Twenty-eighth Street, NW
Washington, DC 20007
(202) 393–4373

Chapter 2
Airline Reservations Agent

Business and vacation travelers want to reach their destinations the fastest and easiest way. They want good service with no worries about how to get there.

The airline reservations agent is the person who helps people with their travel plans. Reservations agents work for one particular airline. They work directly with customers and with travel agencies to arrange flights. To do their job well, they need good communications skills.

Education, Training, and Salary

Most airlines require an airline reservations agent to have a high school education.

New reservations agents are trained on the job by the airline. They usually receive one month of classroom training. Good typing skills and the ability to use a computer are needed for the job. Trainees learn about the airline they will be working for. They learn its policies and rules. They also learn how to use a computer to help them plan trips.

Reservations agents earn about $25,000 a year. Pay raises come with experience. Benefits include low airline fares, paid vacation, medical insurance, and retirement plans.

Job Description

Airline reservations agents book plane reservations for passengers. They usually take reservations by phone. But first they must be sure they have all the necessary information.

Agents ask a number of questions:

- Where will you travel from?
- Where will you travel to?
- What day will you leave?
- What day will you return?

After getting answers to these questions, agents look up flight information on the computer. Then they ask a few more questions:

- What time of day do you want to travel?
- How many people will be traveling?
- Will you need special meals?
- Will you need assistance—wheelchairs or carts—at either airport?

Customers often have other questions for the reservations agent. They may want to know about the lowest fare. They may want to know if there is a nonstop flight.

If there are no seats for the customer's first choice, clerks must check other flights for seats. Sometimes agents cannot find convenient flights on their airline. Then they check into availability on another airline.

Computers are valuable aids to airline reservations agents. These workers use computers to check schedules, to find open seats, and to make and change reservations. Many reservations agents work in different cities reserving seats. They depend on the computer to keep track of all reservations.

22

Talking About the Job

"Your flight, number 366 from Omaha, Nebraska, to Newark, New Jersey, on Sunday, May 22, is confirmed for three passengers in coach. Thank you for calling Northern Airways."

That's a typical conversation for me at work. I'm Jim Williams, and I'm a reservations agent in Chicago. I'm the one you call when you want to make plane reservations to go anywhere that Northern Airways flies.

My job keeps me busy, especially around the holidays, when more people travel. You can probably guess that I never take a vacation during our busy times. In fact, the company often hires extra help during the Christmas and New Year's holidays to handle the extra travelers.

I started out working part time for the airlines when I was in high school. I was an assistant in reservations, which was a good way to learn the business. I learned how to use the computer. In fact, it wasn't as difficult as I had thought.

You know what got me interested in airline work? It was back in school, when our class went on a field trip to O'Hare Airport. Some airline employees took us in the back, and we saw how they ticket passengers, check in bags, assign seats, and load bags onto planes. I was fascinated with airplanes and travel, and that's how I ended up here.

The big reason I like working for the airlines is the travel benefits. We get free tickets or lower fares on some flights. And our families are included, too. I've traveled all over the United States, to Mexico, and to Europe. I'm already planning a trip to Alaska in the spring. I'm glad I got hooked on the airlines back then. It was a good experience for me.

An airline reservations agent must be pleasant and polite to customers on the phone. Being able to speak other languages can be a plus. This is especially true for agents who work for airlines that fly to other countries.

Airline reservations agents work a regular forty-hour week. But they often work holidays and weekends during peak travel seasons. Some work an evening shift. Those who work nights often earn extra pay.

Outlook for Jobs

Agents who gain experience and get good recommendations from their managers may be promoted to supervisory jobs. They can move up to be district sales managers or to other jobs in airline management. Some airlines require senior agents and other high-level workers to take two to four years of college. Some reservations agents become flight attendants.

Airlines, as with other transportation businesses, are affected by the economy. If the economy is slow, people may not spend as much on travel. If airlines lose business, they may have to lay off employees and stop hiring new ones. If the economy is good and people have extra money for travel, airlines may hire more workers to keep up with the extra business.

Airline prices also can affect the industry. When airlines compete by offering lower prices, more people may schedule trips. If airline prices are high, people may put off trips. Some choose to travel by another form of transportation such as car, bus, or train.

Over 100,000 people worked as reservations agents in the late 1980s. Three-quarters of these worked for airlines. Throughout the 1990s, the number of these jobs may not be as large. As computers are used to do more of the scheduling, fewer people will be needed. Most openings will come up as workers transfer or retire. There will be a lot of competition for these airline jobs because of the travel benefits.

For more information on airline reservations agents, write to:

Airline Employees Association, International
5600 South Central Avenue
Chicago, IL 60638
(312) 767–3333

Air Transport Association of America
1709 New York Avenue, NW
Washington, DC 20006
(202) 626–4000

Interested people should also check the classified newspaper ads for job openings. Or they could write a letter to the personnel director at the airline's main office.

Chapter 3
Travel Agent

Travel agents make transportation and hotel or motel plans for their clients. A good travel agent can set up an entire trip. All the customer has to do is show up on time for departure and follow directions to the hotel.

Education, Training, and Salary

A travel agent needs a high school education and must be able to use a computer. College courses in business and accounting are also helpful. Knowing foreign languages can be very useful to agents, who often speak or write to people in other countries.

To become a travel agent, a person should complete a correspondence course or a travel agent training program. Training schools for travel agents can be found in major cities. Many private business schools and adult education programs also offer this training.

Travel agents starting out earn about $11,500 a year. Most agents work on a commission basis. This means that they earn money each time they arrange a trip. The more trips they arrange, the higher their earnings.

Successful travel agents can earn $19,000 or more. Benefits include paid vacations, medical insurance, discounts on transportation and hotels, and retirement plans.

Job Description

There are two kinds of travel agents: wholesale and retail. Wholesale agents arrange tours for large groups. They then sell these tour packages to retail agents, who deal directly with the public. Wholesale agents package a tour by arranging for transportation, hotel, and tour escorts. They establish the trip schedule and identify possible side trips. They must be good salespeople in order to sell these packages to retail agents.

Retail travel agents work in storefronts open to the public. They have the latest travel brochures and timetables for scheduling trips.

The duties of the travel agent depend on the size of the agency. In large agencies, agents may specialize in a certain area of the world, such as Europe. Those agents become experts in what is available for transportation, hotels, and tours. Any client who enters the agency to make arrangements for a European trip is referred to those agents. Agents may also specialize in business travel or in selling tours or cruises.

In smaller agencies, agents' duties would be more general. They would be likely to handle all types of travel to all locations.

Travel agents plan a variety of trips for different types of travelers. They book reservations on ships, airplanes, buses, and trains. They schedule stays at hotels, motels, and resorts. They also arrange for local transportation once customers arrive at their destinations.

When customers are traveling out of the country, the travel agent informs them of passport and visa requirements. They must also be told the rate of exchange for the dollar at the time. If travelers plan to bring goods back into the coun-

Talking About the Job

The first thing I tell people who ask what it takes to be a travel agent is, "You have to love to travel." I really believe that enjoying travel is the key to being a successful travel agent.

I'm Stacy Rettburg and I'm a travel agent at Adventure Travel. I say you have to love to travel because you have to plan a trip as if *you* are taking it. If you get excited about a location, you'll plan it better. You'll take a little more time than if you look at it as just a trip. You have to take a personal interest in people's travel plans.

Take the example of two clients I had, the Gradys. They had saved for a long time to take a nice vacation. They knew they wanted to go someplace warm (it was February), but they didn't know where. I have traveled quite a bit since becoming a travel agent, so I used my experience to help them choose a spot. It was important that I find out what they enjoyed doing—what their idea of a perfect vacation was.

It's so different with everyone. Some people want an action-packed, busy-every-minute trip. Others want peace and relaxation. The Gradys wanted a little of each. I found them a beautiful Caribbean island that was not too developed and not too deserted. It had just enough activity to keep them entertained when they wanted a change from the quiet beaches.

I decided on a travel job when I saw an ad for a travel school in the newspaper. I live in Houston, which is a large city, but I've learned that agencies are found everywhere—even in small towns.

Nina, who also works here, took another route to becoming a travel agent. She took a correspondence course offered by ASTA, the American Society of Travel Agents. It was all handled by mail. She was able to take the course while she worked at her previous job.

So if you think you'd like to be a travel agent, I say go for it. You'll be glad you did.

try, they ask the agent about import duties and laws.

Travel agents take care of all the phone calls, scheduling, typing, and mailing of travel plans.

They check around from airline to airline and from hotel to hotel to find the package that is best for the customer. In the modern travel agency, most of this checking is done using computerized data bases.

Some agents work for automobile clubs, travel charter clubs, or oil companies. Other agents work for federal, state, and local governments. Their job is to help promote tourism.

Outlook for Jobs

Travel agents in small agencies can advance by moving to larger agencies and specializing in an area. They can also become agency directors or start their own agencies. Someone interested in wholesale travel can get good experience leading tour groups.

People are traveling more today than ever before. This trend is expected to continue into the future. The years ahead look excellent for young people hoping to become travel agents. In fact, travel agencies are expected to be one of the ten fastest-growing areas of employment.

For more information on travel agents, write to:

American Society of Travel Agents
1101 King Street
Alexandria, VA 22314
(703) 739–2782

Association of Retail Travel Agents
25 South Riverside
Croton-on-Hudson, NY 10520
(914) 271–4357

Institute of Certified Travel Agents

148 Linden Street
P.O. Box 56
Wellesley, MA 02181
(617) 237–0280

Travel Industry Association of America

Two Lafayette Center
1133 Twenty-first Street, NW
Washington, DC 20036
(202) 293–1433

Interested people can apply directly to travel agencies for jobs. They should also check the classified ads in the newspaper, trade magazines, and journals.

Chapter 4
Limousine Driver and Tour-Bus Driver

Limousine Driver

People who need to get from one place to another sometimes want someone else to do the driving. They may be traveling to or from the airport, to a wedding, to a prom, or to a special event such as a concert. Whatever the reason, these people call a limousine or livery service to take them to their destinations.

Education, Training, and Salary   A high school diploma is not required by all employers. But some limousine companies do ask that a driver have a high school education.

Limousine drivers must have driver's licenses. They must be careful drivers and have safe driving records for at least three years.

Earnings for limousine drivers vary from company to company. They also depend on whether drivers use their own cars or company-owned cars. Drivers earn a percentage of the fares they receive. Those who use their own cars earn about 70 percent of each fare while the company gets 30 percent. Those who drive company-owned cars earn about 40 percent of each fare. The company gets the rest. Drivers who are independent workers must provide their own insurance and other benefits. Drivers who use their own cars use some of their income to keep their cars in good condition. They must also pay for their gasoline.

Job Description   Limousine drivers pick up and bring customers to a variety of places. The most common reason for someone calling a limousine is for a ride to or from an airport. When the destination is an event, drivers often wait while customers attend the event. Working long hours, waiting for hours, and driving short and long distances are the limousine driver's job.

People thinking about becoming limousine drivers should be willing to work long days, very early or very late, and on weekends. They should like dealing with people because they will meet many different customers. They should also enjoy driving since they are in the car constantly.

Limousine drivers get their assignments through the company. Fares are set by the company, too. Clients are told in advance what the fare will be. Drivers are not permitted to get their own assignments or arrange their own fares. Doing so could be grounds for firing.

The limousine driver is responsible for collecting the full fare on an assignment. On returning to the company's office, the driver gives the correct portion of the fare to the company.

Outlook for Jobs   As drivers gain experience and put in time with a company, they are given assignments that pay more. These may be suburb-to-suburb trips where they earn more money for less time spent driving.

Limousine service is a growing industry. More jobs should open up in the future.

Vacationers in Chattanooga learn more about the city's historic sites with the help of a tour guide.

Tour-Bus Driver

Tour-bus drivers take tourists to historic sites or parks. Sometimes they help explain the history of the place. Many of these trips are local and just last a day or less. But trips could also be long distance and take several days.

Education, Training, and Salary

Education requirements vary from company to company. Many employers do not require a tour-bus driver to have a high school education.

Tour-bus drivers must have safe driving records. Under federal law, they must pass a test for drug and alcohol before they can be hired. They must also pass both written and driving tests to earn special commercial licenses.

Tour-bus drivers' earnings differ from company to company. They may earn from $7.00 to $9.00 an hour. Full-time drivers receive benefits like medical insurance, paid vacations, and retirement plans.

Job Description   Tour-bus drivers are in charge of safely bringing passengers to their destinations. The types of trips depend on the company that employs the drivers. They may do a half-day trip taking schoolchildren to a museum or a week-long trip to Florida.

People who want to become tour-bus drivers must like to drive. They should enjoy large groups of people—including noisy children. They must be friendly and polite to passengers and always drive responsibly. They must have patience since the job often requires them to wait and fill the time while passengers attend an event or go sightseeing. Drivers must also be good at directions and finding locations. Many drivers are responsible for mapping their own routes.

The Interstate Commerce Commission (ICC) regulates the motorcoach industry. It has made rules for employees. For instance, no driver can work more than seventy hours in a seven-day period. If they do work seventy hours, they must have some days off. Another rule says that they cannot earn special overtime pay for driving. These rules all help make sure that drivers are rested and can drive buses safely.

Outlook for Jobs   Tour-bus drivers advance by earning raises in pay. There should be plenty of jobs for tour-bus drivers in the future. These are likely to be with large motorcoach companies that are expected to dominate the field. In the future, the smaller independent companies will find it harder to afford the costly insurance that is required.

Many motorcoach companies have a high turnover because workers often quit. This is partly because of the large amount of travel required for bus drivers, often overnight and out of state. All this travel can be difficult for drivers with families.

For more information on limousine drivers and tour-bus drivers, write to:

International Brotherhood of Teamsters, Chauffeurs, Warehousemen and Helpers of America
25 Louisiana Avenue, NW
Washington, DC 20001
(202) 624–6800

Interested people also can apply directly to limousine companies and motorcoach companies for jobs.

Chapter 5
Tour Guide

When vacation travelers are in foreign cities, they are often unsure about how to get around and see the sights. They may not speak the language well. Many want someone to help show them around. Travelers often take organized tours to get the most out of a trip. The people who lead these tours are tour guides.

Education, Training, and Salary

A tour guide must have a high school education. Most tour companies train guides on the job. Trainees learn from working with experienced guides. Tour guides with large tour companies may go through a long training period. This training prepares them for all situations that might arise on a tour.

Guides often lead tours with visitors from other countries. As a result, it is very helpful for a tour guide to speak one or more foreign languages. Knowing about art history, architecture, archeology, and history is also important for a tour guide.

Most tour guides earn about $200 to $500 per week. They may receive tips from travelers. Benefits can include free hotel and travel. Tourism is a seasonal business. As a result, guides may have weeks where there is no work. Larger tour companies may offer benefits to their guides.

Where Tours Go

Area Tours: These trips include travel in such regions as Scandinavia, Alpine Europe, or the British Isles.

Single-Country Tours: Some tours concentrate on one country, including many of those in Europe and Asia.

Two-City Tours: Tours can focus on two important cities, either in the same country (such as Rome and Florence) or in different countries (such as Paris and London).

Single-City Tours: Some tours concentrate on seeing as much as possible of a major city, which may include such important sites as New York City, Los Angeles, Paris, London, Moscow, Mexico City, Rio de Janeiro, Beijing, or Tokyo.

Relaxation Tours: Popular destinations are the Caribbean, Hawaii, Mexico, and the Mediterranean.

Scenic Tours: Locations can include New England in the fall foliage season, French castles, or Canadian or American national parks.

Adventure Tours: Tours include mountaineering in the Himalayas, seeing the Sahara Desert by camel, African safaris, horseback tours of the Canadian Rockies, or white-water rafting in Alaska.

Sports Tours: Packages can include visits to tennis, ski, or golf resorts or attendance at sporting events such as the World Series, the Superbowl, or the Kentucky Derby.

Special-Interest Tours: These include tours built around a theme, such as English country houses or bird-watching.

Job Description

Tour guides lead tourists on trips all over the world. These trips could include a long journey through China or a one-day bus tour. Some tours are inexpensive walks in a museum. Others are religious trips to sacred places. Local tours visit important historical sites. There are a wide variety of tours for every budget and taste.

Tour guides may work for small tour operators or large tour companies. The companies might aim their tours at special groups, such as students or retired people.

Good speaking and listening skills are a must for tour guides. They spend most of their time explaining things and answering questions. They often must memorize a lot of facts about a place in order to inform travelers.

Tour guides must be able to act quickly and intelligently in an emergency. Problems include airline, bus, or train problems; not enough hotel rooms; and lost luggage. Whatever the cause, the tour guide must handle these problems calmly and with authority.

Guides must be very organized since they handle schedules for an entire group. They also must be good at keeping track of expenses.

A tour guide's work can be tiring and demanding. They may have several trips in a row and be away from home for long periods of time. Yet they must be as polite and helpful to the customers on the fifteenth trip as they were on the first. Still, many feel there are more advantages than disadvantages to the job of guide. The excitement of seeing different cities and meeting new people can be rewarding.

Outlook for Jobs

Beginning tour guides start out giving tours of one location only. With experience they move up to taking different groups to different places. Guides start out as trainees helping other guides. As they advance, guides are given more responsibility. They plan and organize their own trips. They can also become tour supervisors.

The travel industry is experiencing high growth, so the outlook for jobs as tour guides is

Talking About the Job

Today, Rome. Next month, London and the English countryside. After that, it's on to Spain and Portugal. That's the life of a tour guide.

I'm Roberto Ramos, and I am a tour guide with Tour Europa. We offer package tours to groups from the United States and other countries. I have been a tour guide for several years now, and it is a good life for me. I love to travel, and now that I have been with the company for a long time, I go to different cities and countries all the time.

I started out working in a museum giving guided tours of the galleries. I gave the same tour several times a day, five days a week. I knew more about sculpture and painting than anyone around. I thought that the job would be good preparation for a job as an overseas guide, so I stayed with it. This job experience looked good on my résumé. And it gave me good experience for what I do now.

I speak Spanish and French. Knowing these languages really helps me get the good assignments. On many tours, I need to repeat what I am saying in more than one language. Knowing these languages also helps me talk to people who work at museums or historic buildings when I work in Europe.

For many guide jobs in the United States, you can get along without another language. This is especially true at places like museums, government buildings, and historic sites. Those are good places to start out if you want to move up to longer tours.

I am thinking about starting my own small tour company sometime in the future. I would specialize in tours of Spain and Portugal for people from other countries. Everybody has to have a dream, right?

excellent. As with other jobs in the travel and tourism field, the number of openings in the future will depend partly on the economy. But there will always be job openings when tour guides move up to other jobs or retire.

For more information on tour guides, write to:

American Society of Travel Agents
1101 King Street
Alexandria, VA 22314
(703) 739–2782

International Association of Tour Managers
1646 Chapel Street
New Haven, CT 06511
(203) 777–5994

National Tour Association
P.O. Box 3071
Lexington, KY 40596
(606) 253–1036

Interested people should look for names and addresses of tour operators in travel brochures and advertisements. They can send letters and résumés to these companies and possibly schedule an interview. Travel directories also have names of tour companies. Check at the public library for more help.

Chapter 6
Taxi Dispatcher

Taxicab drivers drive around on the lookout for passengers. Other times they are given specific assignments to pick up people who have called for a cab. Drivers receive their assignments from the taxi dispatcher over a two-way radio. The dispatcher works at the cab company office.

Education, Training, and Salary

Taxicab companies require that a dispatcher have a high school education. Dispatchers receive their training on the job. First they start out as operators. These workers take incoming calls from people needing taxi service.

Taxi dispatchers start at $6.00 to $7.00 an hour and average about $18,000 a year. Operators earn from $4.25 to $5.00 an hour. With experience they may move up to be dispatcher trainees, who earn $5.25 an hour. Benefits include medical insurance, paid vacations and holidays, and retirement plans.

Job Description

The dispatcher controls where the cabs go to pick up passengers. It is the dispatcher's job to make sure that cabs show up on time at their destinations to pick up passengers.

Most cities are divided into posts, or areas. North-south and east-west streets are used as boundaries to divide the posts. These posts are squares on a big map that the dispatcher uses to give orders to drivers. Each post has a number, and all drivers can go to all posts. Dispatchers send the cab that is nearest to the person who called in.

Dispatchers place orders that come in on a board. This is a large table with a map of the area. Dispatchers must know all the blocks in cities. They must also know all towns in the surrounding area. They must be able to tell if a cab is in the same general area to collect a passenger. There is not enough time to constantly check the map to locate streets. For that reason, a dispatcher needs a good memory.

Dispatchers must speak quickly and clearly so that drivers can understand them over the radio. They might have ten drivers on the radio at one time, each thinking that he or she is the only one receiving an assignment. A quick, sharp mind is a must for a taxi dispatcher.

Dispatchers must act quickly and responsibly in an emergency, too. A driver who is robbed or in a car accident will radio the cab company and announce the problem. The dispatcher quickly gets on the radio to alert all drivers. The dispatcher then asks the driver: "Where are you and what do you need?" As soon as the emergency call comes in, an operator dials 911 and alerts the police. The driver may be hurt or unsure about what to do. If that is the case, the dispatcher often must help.

In many cities, police will not arrive on the scene for a car accident unless someone is injured

Talking About the Job

"Car 601 to 4th and Kedzie, fare to the airport. Car 222 to North Canal and Madison, fare to the Biltmore Hotel. Car 937 to 602 Lexington Avenue, apartment 2A, fare to the airport."

It's a typical day here at City Cab Company. Everybody wants to go everywhere, all at the same time. I'm Letitia Sanborn, and I'm a taxi dispatcher. I've been here four years, and I can't imagine working anywhere else.

I started out here as an operator right after I graduated from high school. I learned a lot watching, listening, taking phone calls, and seeing how experienced dispatchers handle crises. I couldn't have learned any of this from a book or a classroom—nowhere but right here, in the middle of it all.

In a city, cabs are a major form of transportation for a lot of people. The buses aren't always useful since they only make certain stops. And many people who live here don't have cars because it's hard to find parking spaces, and garages are costly. A lot of people who come into the city to work take trains. Then they need rides from the train station. So cabs are always in demand.

I tell anyone who is thinking about becoming a taxi dispatcher that you better like juggling. Juggling phone orders, that is. I send out dozens of orders every couple of minutes, and all the time I have to keep track of where my drivers are. And we often get calls from customers wanting to know where their cab is. The recheck operator follows up on these calls. But sometimes I have to light a fire under the slow drivers or find out what's keeping them. Passengers sometimes hear me yelling at drivers to hurry up or find another route.

I'll say one thing about this job—it's never boring.

or the car is too damaged to be driven. So the dispatcher must tell the driver what to do.

Dispatchers work eight-hour shifts. The shifts last from 7:00 A.M. to 3:00 P.M., from 3:00 P.M. to 11:00 P.M., or from 11:00 P.M. to 7:00 A.M. These

47

shifts are assigned to dispatchers by chance. (Most cab drivers work twelve-hour shifts.)

Dispatchers in cities may handle as many as 4,000 cabs. In the suburbs, twenty or thirty may work for the company, depending on need and the size of the area served.

Operators need good memories, too. They must memorize streets and areas in a short period of time. If they have not been able to do this within about two months, they may not be cut out for the job of taxi dispatcher.

Outlook for Jobs

A high school graduate can walk into a cab company office and apply for a job as an operator and be trained on the job. Operators take all incoming calls for customers and give these orders to the dispatcher. Operators can advance to be recheck operators. These workers handle calls from customers who have not been picked up yet. They then can advance to be dispatcher trainees and learn from an experienced dispatcher.

Taxi dispatcher jobs should be available in the coming years. Many people in cities are using cabs more often because of the rising cost of buses and the difficulty in finding parking.

For more information on taxi dispatchers, write to:

American Society of Transportation and Logistics
P.O. Box 33095
Louisville, KY 40232
(502) 451–8150

International Brotherhood of Teamsters, Chauffeurs, Warehousemen and Helpers of America
25 Louisiana Avenue, NW
Washington, DC 20001
(202) 624–6800

Interested people should also apply at taxicab companies.

Chapter 7
Caterer

Suppose a bank needs to provide food service for its employee cafeteria. It may turn to a catering company that specializes in serving food to large groups of people. A couple planning a wedding reception may turn to a caterer as well. Caterers prepare good-tasting meals for people to enjoy at parties or special events.

Education, Training, and Salary

Most caterers have at least a high school education. Some have attended technical or trade schools and have taken classes in cooking or food service. Many caterers train on the job. Others enter two-year colleges to study food service or business. With a college degree in business, a caterer may become an assistant manager or manager in a large catering company.

For caterers who own their own companies, earnings depend on how much business they can get. Industrial caterers can earn $18,000 or more. These workers prepare food in company cafeterias. Large catering companies often provide benefits such as medical insurance, paid vacations, and retirement plans. Caterers who are employed by major companies in their lunchrooms get whatever benefits those companies provide to all of their workers. Caterers who are self-employed must have their own benefits.

Job Description

Caterers often are creative people. They enjoy putting together tasty and good-looking tables of food. They know that food is more enjoyable if it not only tastes good but also looks appealing.

Owners of small catering companies may do everything themselves. They make special meals for luncheons and dinner parties. They may cook the food in their own kitchens and bring it to the customer's home. Or they may do all the cooking in the customer's kitchen. Caterers or their helpers may serve the food and handle the cleanup also.

Small catering firms sometimes hire outside helpers. These workers include waiters and waitresses, bartenders, and extra cooks. Companies hire these workers when they cook for large dinners such as weddings, banquets, and other events.

Large catering firms provide food service to hospitals, company cafeterias, college dining halls, schools, sports arenas, and convention centers. Caterers who work in such places have contracts to provide food service for a year or more. These companies have many managers, assistant managers, food preparers, and servers on staff.

Caterers must find their own business contacts. They get work by advertising their services. Or they get new clients by word of mouth from satisfied customers. To succeed, these caterers must also be good businesspeople. They must work on a budget, keeping track of how much money goes out to buy supplies and how much comes in. They must know where to buy good-quality supplies at the lowest prices.

Caterers provide a variety of delicious, attractively arranged dishes for special occasions.

It takes experience and skill to know how much food and other supplies to order for a group. This planning is a large part of the caterer's job.

Caterers must also be good managers of people. They supervise their staffs and make sure that each member does his or her job correctly. And they must be able to deal well with their customers. It is often difficult to please some customers, but the caterer must do everything possible. This may include creating unusual food and decorations. Caterers may mold food in the shapes of animals, bake fancy wedding cakes, cook special foreign dishes, and make ice sculptures. There are many possibilities, and the successful caterer is willing to try most of them.

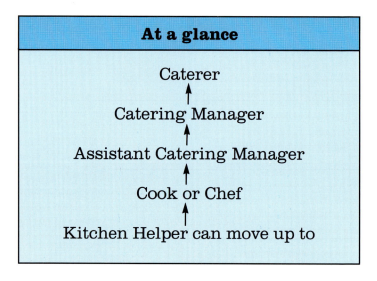

At a glance
Caterer
↑
Catering Manager
↑
Assistant Catering Manager
↑
Cook or Chef
↑
Kitchen Helper can move up to

Another type of caterer cooks food for coin-operated vending machines at public buildings, hospitals, or offices. They may offer hot and cold foods, using small microwave ovens to heat the meals. Mobile caterers drive well-stocked trucks to construction sites, factories, and other places. They serve breakfast or lunch to workers.

Outlook for Jobs

People interested in becoming caterers can start out in any job in food service where they can learn about food and cooking equipment. They might start out as kitchen helpers, cutting up foods or assisting cooks in other ways. Next they might become cooks themselves and train in food preparation. With enough training and skill, they might become chefs. With a business education, they might move up higher. They could become assistant catering managers or catering managers. Further advancement might come by moving to a larger catering firm.

Some people want to start up their own catering companies. They need enough money and good business sense.

The job outlook for small caterers through the year 2000 is good. There is much competition from existing companies and new ones starting up all the time. But the food-service industry is expected to continue its boom, so catering will still be popular. Large companies will also be hiring caterers to provide food service to companies and schools.

For more information on caterers, write to:

International Food Service Executives Association
3017 West Charleston Boulevard
Las Vegas, NV 89102
(702) 878–2029

Mobile Industrial Caterers Association
7300 Artesia Boulevard
Buena Park, CA 90621
(714) 521–6000

People interested in jobs in the catering business can apply directly to catering companies. They should also check employment agencies or state employment services for job openings. Newspapers also advertise catering job opportunities.

Chapter 8
Truck-Stop Operator

Many jobs in travel and tourism depend on other workers. Long-distance truck drivers spend most of their time on the state highways and interstates of this country. Nearly 2.5 million truck drivers carry one-quarter of the nation's freight each year. Truckers have time schedules to meet. They need fast, convenient services when they are on the road. Workers in truck stops provide food, clean rest rooms, service centers for trucks, and stores that sell convenience items to truckers. Truck drivers depend on these convenient stops along the highways that link their pickup and destination points. The truck-stop operator manages all the workers, making sure that they provide good service.

Education, Training, and Salary

Most truck stops require that the operator have a high school education. Truck-stop operators can train on the job. Some operators may have useful skills learned in other jobs. These jobs could include work in the food-service industry, in retail stores, or in service stations.

Truck-stop operators can earn from $30,000 to $50,000 per year. The amount depends on their ability and experience and on the size of the truck stop. Independent truck stops may offer different salaries than those owned by chains.

Job Description

Truck-stop operators may also be called general managers. That title sums up their jobs. They have to manage all operations at the truck stop. This duty means that they must be fully in charge of all services that the truck stop offers to its customers.

Truck-stops are open twenty-four hours a day, seven days a week. Truckers pull in for a meal and a rest at all times. That means that the operator, or someone else in charge, must be on duty at all times. The stop needs a staff of other workers at all times as well. Night crews may be smaller if there is usually less business at night.

Truck-stop operators manage all the workers at the stop. They make the schedules for all workers to follow. The workers they supervise include those who work in the food-service, janitorial, store, and service-station areas. Operators must be aware of state labor laws. They must also make sure that their workers follow the rules of the company.

In the restaurant, truck-stop operators must hire people to work as cashiers, waiters or waitresses, cooks, and dishwashers. Operators may be in charge of ordering supplies for the restaurant. They need to track the amount of food that is bought and how much is cooked and eaten. They must be sure to order enough food but not too much. They need to have enough on hand to meet the demands of hungry truckers.

Most truck stops offer private showers for truckers. If drivers buy fuel, the showers can be used free of charge. If no purchase is made, the trucker has to pay a fee to use the shower. The cost could run from $5.00 to $10.00. The truck-

Truckers depend on the special services provided at truck stops when they are on the road.

stop operator must make sure that the stop's cleaning crew keeps the showers clean at all times.

Convenience stores, or travel centers, are an important service at truck stops. These stores provide supplies for truck drivers. They also sell magazines or books, snack foods, and other items. Unlike convenience stores in your neighborhood, these stores sell truck parts and accessories, clothing, and personal items. The operator must hire the staff for the store and oversee its operation.

Maybe the most important part of the truck stop is the service station. There truckers get fuel for their rigs. These stations are usually run by independent suppliers. The operator contracts with the supplier to provide gasoline, oil, and other services. The supplier buys fuel from one of the major oil companies. Operators must make sure that the workers of the service-station area treat the truck drivers—and the trucks—well. Truckers will drive past a truck stop if it provides poor service.

Truck stops must have enough parking space for the large eighteen-wheelers and tractor trailers that park for a short time or for the night. These areas are also maintained by the operator.

As you can see, truck-stop operators must be able to handle many jobs. In a large truck stop, they must supervise many workers and keep track of many different areas. They must know about hiring practices, salaries, benefits, supplies, and much more.

Many of the operators' duties involve money. For this reason, operators must be good with math. They need to control costs and the prices they charge truckers so that the truck stop makes a profit.

Operators also may be involved in advertising their facilities. They need to decide how best to tell the public about their stop and what services they offer. Most of this advertising is done by posting signs along the highway.

Outlook for Jobs

Work in other restaurant or retail jobs is good experience for becoming a truck-stop operator. Supervisory experience can be helpful as well. It trains the operator for the management parts of the job. Taking courses in business will help the operator do the job well.

There is competition for operators' jobs since there is only one general manager's position at each stop. Workers in any of the stop's areas who work hard and show ability may become supervisors in their area. If they show even more ability, they may be put in charge of one of the shifts, when the operator is off duty.

Despite the competition, jobs in truck-stop operation will be available in the coming years. The demand for truck drivers is expected to grow by 20 percent by the year 2000. So there will be a rise in the number of truck stops. Also, stops already in operation will grow. This growth may create more supervisory jobs.

For more information on truck-stop operators, write to:

American Truck Stop Operators Association
P.O. Box 25866
Winston-Salem, NC 27144-5866
(919) 768–4224

Interested people should also apply directly to truck stops for jobs.

Chapter 9
Convention Planner

Conventions take place at large hotels, convention centers, and resorts. People gather from all across the country for meetings. Examples are math teachers, computer workers, or book publishers. Any group with a common interest can hold a convention.

The groups that stage these conventions need the help of experienced people to make all the arrangements. They turn to convention planners to arrange all the details so that their conventions are successful.

Education, Training, and Salary

A convention planner should have a high school education.

It is necessary to have some training to become a convention planner. Hotel or motel management, public relations, or travel and tourism all give a good background for this job.

Salaries vary from company to company. Convention planners with training and experience earn up to $37,000 a year. For convention planners who work independently, earnings depend on how much business they can get. Benefits for planners employed by companies include medical insurance and paid vacations and holidays. Independent convention planners, who work for themselves, must take care of their own benefits.

63

Job Description

A company or group that wants to sponsor a convention hires a convention planner. Planners are in charge of all the arrangements. They perform the following tasks:

- They schedule travel and book hotel rooms.
- They book the facilities (hotel, convention center, or resort).
- They settle on the cost of the facility with its manager.
- They figure out how much space is needed for the event.
- They arrange the main event.
- They get and set up all the audiovisual or other equipment that will be needed.
- They order food service.
- They organize any other services such as child care, entertainment, or sightseeing tours that will be needed.

Convention planners handle all the details for everything except the actual program.

Planners need to consult often with the group staging the convention. They need to confirm their plans and pass information along. For instance, they need to inform the group what hotels they have booked. That way the group's members can be told where to make reservations.

People who want to become convention planners should be very organized and good with details. They must be able to communicate well with clients, suppliers, and managers. They must understand the size and range of an event and plan around its specific needs.

Talking About the Job

6:00 A.M. Booth delivery and setup.

7:00 A.M. Meet with food service.

8:30 A.M. Call equipment rental to check on order.

10:00 A.M. Get final head count for conference.

And that's just this morning. Hi, I'm Teri Leonhardt, and my job is planning conventions. I plan them for every kind of group you can think of. This year, I've arranged conventions for a health-care expo, a group of psychiatrists from the Midwest, foreign language teachers, book publishers, and the electronics industry.

I find the work challenging because I deal with so many different kinds of people. I am right in the middle, dealing with many kinds of industries, rental agencies, hotels, food-service firms, carpenters, airlines, tour buses, and baby-sitting services. And that's not all.

I started out working part time in a travel agency, helping out the employees. I decided in high school that I'd like to work in travel and tourism, so I took the first job I could get in the field. I also worked a couple of summers during high school in a small resort. I organized activities and events for the guests. My guidance counselor at school always said, "Learn all you can from people in the industry." So I always kept my eyes and ears open.

Just from working in those places, I found out a lot about tours, airlines, buses, trains, and hotels. And that knowledge has helped me in convention planning. Now I work for a planning firm. Companies call us to help them with all the arrangements needed for putting together a convention. Sometimes I travel to other cities to check out hotels and convention centers. In fact, I always have to be ready to go at a moment's notice. The job suits me, and I love it.

Some convention planners work for city, county, or state tourist bureaus. They help bring visitors and conventions to the area. These planners must be very familiar with the area and what it has to offer to out-of-state visitors. They often compete with planners from other cities in their efforts to book a convention.

Planners must be willing to work odd hours, since it often is not a 9:00-to-5:00 job. They may have to work evenings and weekends. They often need to travel to convention sites in other cities and states in order to set up events.

A convention planner works with a convention consultant from a travel agency, convention service company, or tourist bureau. Consultants can help suggest places, activities, and arrangements. They may also advertise the event to people who may be interested in attending.

Outlook for Jobs

High school graduates who have no background in the field may start out as secretaries and receptionists for a company that does convention planning. This is a good way to become introduced to the field. By working closely with convention planners, they can learn the business.

Some planners start their own consulting firms. Of course, this takes business knowledge and enough money to begin a new company. Planners who work for city or state convention bureaus move up by being promoted. Those who work for planning companies may also be promoted. If so, they may head up a department.

The future for people seeking jobs as convention planners looks very good. Conventions are more popular than ever and will continue to grow in number. As a result, convention planners will be in demand as we near the year 2000. Conventions also are good business for the cities that host them. These events bring more visitors and dollars into the communities. As a result, the demand for skilled planners will grow.

For more information on convention planners, write to:

International Association of Convention and Visitor Bureaus
P.O. Box 758
Champaign, IL 61820
(217) 359–8881

Meeting Planners International
Infomart Building
1950 Stemmons Freeway
Dallas, TX 75207
(214) 746–5222

People interested in becoming convention planners for city, state, or county tourist bureaus should also check civil service job listings. Trade journals for travel and tourism might list convention jobs with private companies.

Chapter 10
Bookkeeper, Secretary, and Clerk

Clerical jobs in the travel and tourism industry are important. These workers keep offices running smoothly. Bookkeepers, secretaries, and clerks often are the ones who handle all the paperwork and record keeping that goes on behind the scenes. Working in these jobs can be a great way for interested people to learn the field. Many travel workers launch their careers with clerical jobs.

Education, Training, and Salary

A high school education is required to do clerical work in travel and tourism.

Applicants will have a big advantage if they have very good typing and filing skills, know how to use most business machines, and are good at keeping things in order. Secretaries must know business English and should know shorthand. Bookkeepers should know business math. On-the-job training is offered in some firms.

Bookkeepers and secretaries earn an average of $11,000 to $18,000 a year. Clerks' salaries vary depending on the kind of work they do and the company they work for. Benefits for all these workers include medical insurance, paid vacations and holidays, and retirement plans.

Job Description

Bookkeepers perform accounting jobs to keep money matters in order. They work for all kinds of businesses and institutions. They handle the money a business spends and the money that is earned. Bookkeepers may help in preparing income tax reports.

Bookkeepers may be hired by motels, hotels, restaurants, and other businesses in the travel and tourism industry. In small companies, a general bookkeeper may run the department and keep all financial records. The work may be done by hand or with such machines as calculators or computers. The bookkeeper may also answer phones and file papers.

In larger companies, a group of bookkeepers and accounting clerks may be supervised by an accountant. Each may be assigned a separate job. These duties include payroll, making checks, doing taxes, and recording documents.

Bookkeepers must work very accurately. The numbers that they enter in the business's books must be correct. These numbers are used to determine how much cash the company has and whether the company is in good financial health. Also, the information that they write down determines how much workers are paid. And their records show how much a client or customer has paid to the company. Errors in payroll or payment records can make workers or clients upset. Errors could even lose money for the company. Working carefully and checking all work for accuracy are important parts of the job.

In some offices, secretaries organize all work done in an office. They may answer the phone, type letters, make appointments, and schedule meetings. They normally do other office work, too, such as filing, typing, and keeping records.

Managers rely on their secretaries to tell them about appointments that are coming up and phone calls that have come in. Many bosses rely on their secretaries to follow up on problems. Secretaries sometimes write letters for their bosses as well. A secretary who can take on these tasks helps the boss greatly.

Secretaries must also be well organized. Managers often work on many projects at the same time. They may want an update of some information, or they may need to get a letter from a file. By having well-organized files, secretaries can get the information quickly.

As with bookkeepers, secretaries must work carefully and accurately. The letters and memos they type should be neat and clean. Accurate, neat work makes a good impression on the company's customers. It also helps impress bosses and may lead to the secretary being given more responsibility.

Some secretaries are also stenographers. They are trained to take dictation. They may do this by using shorthand, a way of copying messages quickly by writing down symbols and letters rather than writing entire words. Or they may work from dictation machines, in which they listen to tapes made by their bosses. In that case, they type out letters while they listen.

Clerk-typists have many duties. They type up bills, reports, and records. They may also act as receptionists and run the copying machine. As they show that they are good workers and well organized, they are given more and more responsibility.

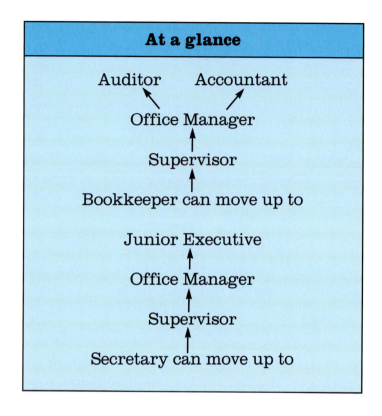

At a glance

Auditor   Accountant

Office Manager

Supervisor

Bookkeeper can move up to

Junior Executive

Office Manager

Supervisor

Secretary can move up to

Outlook for Jobs

Young people can get valuable clerical experience by taking part-time jobs in offices. They can help out filing, typing, answering phones, and assisting full-time workers. Secretaries may be promoted to be supervisors, office managers, or junior executives. Bookkeepers may advance to accounting work with more responsibility and higher pay.

There is often a high turnover in clerical jobs, leaving openings for new workers. As businesses and industries grow, more clerical workers will be needed to keep offices in order. However, with the increase in the use of machines and computers, the number of workers needed may decrease some. Most job openings will be for bookkeeping and accounting clerks.

For more information on bookkeepers, secretaries, or clerks, write to:

**Association of Independent Colleges and
  Schools**
One Dupont Circle, NW
Suite 350
Washington, DC 20036

Interested people can also apply directly to companies where they would like to work. They should check the classified ads for job openings. They can also call state employment offices and private agencies.

Chapter 11
Cruise Director

Passengers on cruise ships look forward to having an enjoyable trip. This may mean different things to different people. To some, it means a quiet, relaxing cruise, sitting on deck and soaking up the sun. To others, doing vigorous exercise, visiting exciting ports of call, or dancing until dawn make a good vacation. The cruise director is the person responsible for making sure that all people on board a cruise ship—whatever their taste in fun—have a memorable experience. A cruise director must plan a wide variety of activities.

Education, Training, and Salary

Most cruise lines prefer that a cruise director have at least a high school education.

Often cruise directors start out as entertainers, athletic directors, or other staff members on board the ship. This is good training for the job of cruise director. Getting to know the specific facilities of the ship is important training for a cruise director as well.

Cruise directors can earn anywhere from $500 a week on a small ship to $2,500 a week on a large ship. Earnings for the year also depend on the number of weeks that the cruise director works. Cruise directors receive such benefits as sleeping accommodations and free meals aboard ship.

A cruise director helps passengers board small rafts for a day trip off the coast of Italy.

Job Description

The cruise director's job is to organize the many activities that are scheduled each day on board a cruise ship. They plan sports, exercise, trips to ports, dances, entertainment, classes, and much more. Their goal is to keep passengers happy and busy. They might set up aerobics classes, swimming lessons, dance lessons, a volleyball tournament, a juggling exhibition, or a limbo contest during the day. Or they might arrange a dinner dance, talent show, celebrity entertainers, or movies for the evening. The cruise director posts events on a daily calendar board and in the ship's newspaper. Events are usually announced over loudspeakers as well.

The cruise director is a manager, in charge of the entertainment staff and all performers. He or she oversees all social events, making sure that they take place on time and as planned. If an event is canceled, the cruise director must arrange to substitute some other activity to take its place.

76

Popular Types of Cruises

Cruise directors plan many different activities. Some are based on the location of the cruise. Some sample cruises are:

Adventure Cruise: Passengers might leave the cruise ship in rubber boats and head for a deserted island off the coast of Chile. Or they might sail down the Amazon River in South America or to the Great Barrier Reef off the coast of Australia. Trips often are physically challenging. Imagine spending nights in a damp rain forest or on a boat in heavy rapids!

Exotic Cruise: Passengers cruise to foreign lands and learn about the region, its people, and its culture. These cruises may go to places with names like Tarawa, Funafuti, Truk, or Ifaluk, beautiful islands in the South Pacific with deep blue lagoons and thatched houses.

California Cruise: Passengers sail on weekend cruises from coastal California cities to ruggedly beautiful Catalina Island, San Diego, or even to Mexico. They may visit ports each day for sightseeing, exploring, and shopping.

Family Cruise: This may be a cruise to the Caribbean. Families are provided with baby-sitters and activities for children such as movies, beach parties, and snorkeling.

Alaska Cruise: An Alaska cruise could include a close-up look at natural, unspoiled land. Passengers may enjoy the sight of dolphins, seals, whales, and bald eagles. Trips may include a cruise to Glacier Bay or Misty Fjords National Monument.

Fitness Cruise: Aerobic workouts; daily swims; and nutritious, low-calorie meals are part of popular "cruise-while-you-lose" fitness cruises. So many adults have become health conscious that some spas and cruise companies offer fitness cruises that even have bike trips when passengers go on shore to visit ports.

Day trips to ports of call are scheduled by cruise directors, who inform passengers of the stops that will be made. They may organize tours in town and hire a tour guide to lead them.

On a small ship, cruise directors may perform many jobs themselves. On large ships, they may oversee fifty or more workers, including the sports and exercise staff, entertainers, and instructors.

Cruise directors live on board ship during the length of the cruise. The cruise may last one week or a whole month. They may work up to sixteen hours a day, every day. Overseeing both daytime and nighttime events means being on duty most of the time. This might not be the job for someone with a family. Most cruise directors are single. They may live on board ship for six to nine months a year.

A ship's steward helps the cruise director by tending to passengers' needs.

Outlook for Jobs

Staff members on board ship can advance to become cruise directors with the right background and training. They can first become assistant cruise directors or cruise directors on small ships. With more experience, a cruise director can move to a larger ship with more responsibility and a higher salary. Cruise directors who want to transfer back to land may take jobs in management at a cruise line's main office.

The popularity of cruises is growing, with about 2 million people going aboard each year. Cruise directors will always be in demand. But the small number of directors' jobs will create much competition for these openings.

For more information on cruise directors, write to:

Travel Industry Association of America
Two Lafayette Center
1133 Twenty-first Street, NW
Washington, DC 20036
(202) 293–1433

Interested people can also apply directly to cruise lines for jobs.

Chapter 12
Getting the Job: Tips for the Reader

Starting Out

Whatever job you decide to go after, you want to do it to the best of your ability. And you can do this only if you have picked a job you enjoy and feel comfortable with. Be honest with yourself and begin your job search by knowing your talents and interests.

Rate Your Strengths

Write down on a piece of paper a few lines about yourself: what you like, what you dislike, what your favorite subject at school is, what your least favorite subject is, what bores you, what excites you.

Make a chart and list any jobs you have ever had. Include your supervisors' names, your work addresses, and the dates of employment. Now make a list of your hobbies or interests. Also list the schools you have attended and your extracurricular activities. This list would include clubs or teams you belong to. If you have done any volunteer work, be sure to list it. Finally, add to your list the names of any awards or prizes that you have won.

List Your Job Possibilities

List all the jobs in this book that sound interesting. Look at each job and see if you qualify. If a job you like requires extra training, write that down. Also check the publications in the back of this book and note the titles of any books or other materials that will tell you more about the jobs you like.

Look at your job list and your strengths list. See where they match up, and put a star by those jobs that would use your strengths.

Consult Counselors

Talk to a guidance counselor at your school about jobs that are open in your field of interest. Your state or local employment service can also help you.

Looking for Work

When you have settled on the jobs you would like, start looking for openings. Apply for as many jobs as you can—the more you apply for, the better your chance of finding one.

Research   Find out everything you can about jobs you are applying for. The more information you have about jobs, employers, and employers' needs, the more impressive you will be in your interview.

Ads   There are two types of newspaper classified ads: *help wanted* and *situation wanted*. A help-wanted ad is placed by an employer looking for a worker to fill a specific job. It tells you the job, requirements, salary, company, and whom to contact. Or it is a blind ad, one that just has a post office box number. Answer the ad by letter or by phone, as directed in the ad. Follow up within two weeks with another phone call or letter if you have not heard from the employer.

A person looking for work can place a situation-wanted ad. This ad tells the kind of work the person is looking for, why he or she qualifies, and when he or she could start working.

Networking   Networking is letting everyone know what jobs you're looking for. Talk to people in your field of interest, friends, or relatives who might be able to help. Some good leads on jobs can be found this way. Follow up on what you learn with a phone call or letter.

Classified Ads—Help Wanted

TOUR GUIDE WANTED The Museum of Sculpture is looking for a part-time guide to work Saturdays and Sundays. No experience necess., will train. Call Mr. Washburn at 555-9999 for an interview.

TRAVEL AGENT World Travel Inc., a s.w. suburban friendly leisure travel agency, PT, flexible hours. 1 yr. agency or airline experience necessary. Sales bg preferred. Call Betty 555-4433 bet 9 and 5.

Secretary — EXECUTIVE ASSISTANT Extremely busy executive of a north side area manufacturing company needs a detail-oriented professional whose personality is outmatched only by their secretarial skills. Type 60wpm, shorthand, word processing. Salary is commensurate with experience. P.O. Box 566, Westwood, CA 90000

DRIVER/limousine FT/PT. Must have exp., knowledge of SW subs. req. (601)555-4499.

DISPATCHER Minneapolis company is seeking to train a full-time dispatcher. Must be able to handle pressure and be willing to grow with a young company. Health, dental, life insurance, profit sharing, vacation pay, and much more. Apply in person only, Mon–Thurs, 7am–7pm. No phone calls. 1001 Operator Blvd., Minneapolis.

Employment Services   Check with the high school's or vocational school's placement service for job openings. State and local employment services often have job listings.

Abbreviations

People who place classified ads often use abbreviated words to make an ad as short as possible. Read the classified-ad section in your newspaper to become familiar with abbreviations. Here is a short list to help you now:

excel — excellent		f.t.	
bnfts. — benefits		or f/t — full time	
exp — experience		emp. — employment	
p.t.		gd. — good	
or p/t — part time		refs. — references	
h.s. — high school		ext. — extension	
grad — graduate		req. — required	
w. — with		sal. — salary	
avail. — available			

Civil Service   Federal, state, and local governments offer many jobs in community services. Find the civil service office near you and inquire. See the feature on the top of the next page. It explains more about civil service exams.

Unions   Find out about labor unions that may be involved with jobs in the field of community services. Check with union locals in your town; you can get phone numbers by asking a librarian.

Temporary Employment   Working on a temporary basis can lead to other jobs or to part-time or full-time work.

Civil Service

Federal and state governments employ several million workers. In order to get a government job, you must first check with the Federal Job Information Center or a state department of personnel office for an announcement concerning the type of job that interests you. The announcement describes the job as well as the education and experience that all applicants will need to be qualified for the job.

Once you know about a government job opening, you must fill out an application to take a civil service test. If your application is approved, you must then take and pass the exam. Exams are usually written, but may also be oral. Some exams include essays or performance tests. All exams are tailored to fit a specific job. An exam may cover such items as English usage, reasoning, or clerical or mechanical skills.

Applying in Person

Applying to a company in person can be a good idea. Call for an appointment and tell the human resources officer that you would like to have an interview. Some employers may ask that you send a letter or résumé first.

Sending Letters

Writing letters to companies can be an effective way to ask about jobs. Typed letters are preferred, but neat, handwritten letters are acceptable. Check the yellow pages or industry magazines at the public library for companies' addresses. The reference librarian can help you. Address letters to the company's personnel or human resources department. Send your résumé with the letter. Keep copies of all letters and follow up in two weeks with another letter.

Résumé

A résumé is a useful one-page outline of information about you that introduces you to a possible future employer. Based on your strengths list, it summarizes your education, work history, and skills.

You will enclose your résumé in letters you write possible employers. You also will take it with you to give to your interviewer. Look at the sample résumé on page 87 to see how a typical résumé looks.

Always put your full name, address, and phone number at the top of the résumé. Type the résumé, if possible, or write it by hand neatly. Then state your objective or the job you are applying for. Put down any experience that shows you are a good worker. Volunteer work and part-time jobs tell an employer that you are always looking to help out and work hard. Put down your most recent job first.

Finally, include information about your education. You can also list any special skills, awards, or honors you have received.

Writing Letters

When you send your résumé in the mail, always attach a cover letter. Your letter will be short, no more than two or three paragraphs. It should come right to the point and lead the employer to your résumé.

Explain what job you are interested in, and include a short listing of your qualifications. Your letter should catch the employer's interest so that the employer wants to turn to your résumé. See the sample on page 88.

Jennifer R. Lanscan
122 Elm Street
Largo, Florida 33540
(813) 555–1212

Objective: Position as secretary.

Experience

1989　　　Helped out in First Methodist Church
　　　　　office during the summer. Did filing,
　　　　　typing, mailings, bulletins.

1988–89　Volunteered to type monthly PTA
　　　　　newsletter for Fieldcrest Elementary
　　　　　School.

Training
High school typing classes. Shorthand course,
1989. Computer training course at Business Jobs
Institute, 1990.

Education
1990　　　Graduated North High School.

References available on request.

March 24, 1991
Peter V. Salace
57 Roundtree
Longmeadow, MA 02111

Mr. Paul Porter
Travel America, Inc.
222 West Parkway
Lester, OK 55555

Dear Mr. Porter:

I am looking for a job as a travel agent. I have heard that Travel America may be hiring one in the near future. As my résumé shows, I have experience in the travel field. I am a hard worker and eager to learn. I am available to work extended hours, evenings, and weekends.

I would welcome the opportunity to meet with you and discuss my background and how I can help Travel America.

Thank you for your time. I look forward to hearing from you.

Sincerely,

Peter V. Salace

enclosure

Completing the Application Form

You may have to fill out an application form when applying for a job. (See the sample on pages 90 and 91.) This form asks for your education, experience, work history, and possibly other information.

The employer may mail an application form to you ahead of time or you may be asked to fill it in when you come for the interview.

Follow the instructions carefully and print or type information neatly. Neatness tells the employer that you care about work, can organize information, and that you can think clearly.

Have all information with you when you arrive. You may have to fill in salaries for past jobs, your social security number, the dates you worked, and your past supervisors' names, addresses, and phone numbers.

List your most recent jobs first, as you do on your résumé.

However, do not answer any question that you feel invades your privacy. Laws prevent an employer from asking about race, religion, national origin, age, marital status, family situation, property, car, or arrest record. Unless the question applies directly to the job, you do not have to answer it. (See "Know Your Rights.")

The Interview

How you present yourself in a job interview will tell the employer a lot about you. It can be the biggest single factor that helps an employer decide whether to hire you. The information required is similar to that listed on your résumé, but the employer uses a standard form for all applicants.

APPLICATION FOR EMPLOYMENT

(Please print or type your answers)

PERSONAL INFORMATION   Date _____

Name _____ Social Security Number _____ / _____ / _____

Address _____
     Street and Number   City   State   Zip Code

Telephone number (_____) _____ – _____ (_____) _____ – _____
          day   evening

Job applied for _____ Salary expected $ _____ per _____

How did you learn of this position? _____

Do you want to work _____ Full time or _____ Part time?

Specify preferred days and hours if you answered part time _____

Have you worked for us before? _____ If yes, when? _____

On what date will you be able to start work? _____

Have you ever been convicted of a crime, excluding misdemeanors and summary offenses?

_____ No   _____ Yes

If yes, describe in full _____

Whom should we notify in case of emergency?

Name _____ Relationship _____

Address _____
     Street and number   City   State   Zip Code

Telephone number (_____) _____ – _____ (_____) _____ – _____
          day   evening

EDUCATION

Type of School	Name and Address	Years Attended	Graduated	Course or Major
High School			Yes No	
College			Yes No	
Post-graduate			Yes No	
Business or Trade			Yes No	
Military or other			Yes No	

WORK EXPERIENCE (List in order, beginning with most recent job)

Dates		Employer's Name and Address	Rate of Pay Start/Finish	Position Held	Reason for Leaving
From	To				

ACTIVITIES AND HONORS (List any academic, extracurricular, civic, or other achievements you consider significant.)

PERSONAL REFERENCES

Name and Occupation   Address   Phone Number

PLEASE READ THE FOLLOWING STATEMENTS CAREFULLY AND SIGN BELOW:

The information that I have provided on this application is accurate to the best of my knowledge and is subject to validation. I authorize the schools, persons, current employer, and other organizations or employers named in this application to provide any relevant information that may be required to arrive at an employment decision.

Applicant's Signature   Date

Before you go to the interview, sit down and prepare what you will say. Think of why you want the job, your experience, and why you qualify. Know as much about the job and the company as possible through ads, brochures, or employees. This will show that you are interested in the company's needs.

Make a list of questions you have. And try to guess what the interviewer will ask. You may ask if you can work overtime or if you can take courses for more training or education. Bring in any certificates or licenses you may need to show.

Dress neatly and appropriately for the interview. Make sure you know exactly where the interview will take place so you will be on time. Allow extra time to get there in case you are delayed by traffic or for some other reason.

Following Up

After the interview, thank the interviewer for his or her time and shake hands. If the job appeals to you, tell the person that you are interested.

When you get back home, send a letter thanking the interviewer for his or her time. Repeat things that were discussed in the interview. Keep a copy of it for yourself and start a file for all future letters.

Think about how you acted in the interview. Did you ask the right questions? Were your answers right? If you feel you should have done something differently, make notes so you can do better the next time.

If you do not hear from the company in two weeks, write a letter to the interviewer repeating your interest. You can also phone to follow up.

Know Your Rights: What Is the Law?

Federal   Under federal law, employers cannot discriminate on the basis of race, religion, sex, national origin, ancestry, or age. People aged forty to seventy are specifically protected against age discrimination. Handicapped workers also are protected. Of course, these laws protect only applicants who are qualified or workers who do their jobs. Employers are able to turn down people who do not have needed skills. And they have the right to fire workers who do not perform.

State   Many states have laws against discrimination based on age, handicap, or membership in armed services reserves. Laws differ from state to state. In some states, there can be no enforced retirement age. And some protect people suffering from AIDS.

Applications   When filling out applications, you do not have to answer questions that may discriminate. Questions about whether you are married, have children, own property or a car, or have an arrest record do not have to be answered. An employer may ask, however, if you have ever been convicted of a crime.

At Work   It is against the law for employers to discriminate against workers when setting hours, workplace conditions, salary, hirings, layoffs, firings, or promotions. And no employer can treat a worker unfairly if he or she has filed a discrimination suit or taken other legal action.

Read Your Contract   Read any work contract you are given. Do not sign it until you understand and agree to everything in it. Ask questions if you have them. If you have used an employment agency, before you sign a contract, settle on whether you pay the fee for finding a job or the employer does.

When Discrimination Occurs: What You Can Do

Government Help   Call the Equal Employment Opportunity Commission or the state civil rights commission if you feel you've been discriminated against. If they think you have been unfairly treated, they may take legal action. If you have been unfairly denied a job, you may get it. If you have been unfairly fired, you may get your job back and receive pay that is owed you. Any mention of the actions taken against you may be removed from your work records. To file a lawsuit, you will need a lawyer.

Private Help   Private organizations like the American Civil Liberties Union (ACLU) and the National Association for the Advancement of Colored People (NAACP) fight against discrimination. They can give you advice.

Sources

General Career Information

Career Information Center, 4th ed., 13 vols. Mission Hills, Calif.: Glencoe/Macmillan, 1990.

Harrington, Thomas, and O'Shea, Arthur (eds.). *Guide for Occupational Exploration.* Circle Pines, Minn.: American Guidance Service, 1984.

Hopke, William E., et al. (eds.). *The Encyclopedia of Career and Vocational Guidance,* 7th ed., 3 vols. Chicago: Ferguson, 1987.

U.S. Department of Labor. *Occupational Outlook Handbook.* Washington, D.C.: U.S. Government Printing Office, revised biennially.

Travel and Tourism

Grant, Edgar. *Exploring Careers in the Travel Industry.* New York: Rosen Publishing Group, 1987.

Lawrence, Elizabeth. *The Complete Caterer.* New York: Doubleday, 1988.

Petteway, Van H. *How to Succeed as a Travel Agent.* Plattsburgh, N.Y.: Worldwide Travel, 1985.

Rubin, Karen. *Flying High in Travel: A Complete Guide to Careers in the Travel Industry.* New York: Wiley, 1986.

Stevens, Laurence. *Your Career in Travel and Tourism.* Wheaton, Ill.: Merton House, 1985.

Index

Ads in newspapers, 25, 31,
  82–83
Airline reservations agent,
  21–25; management jobs,
  24
Airlines growth, 11
Apartment house doorman,
  18–19
Application, making, 81–91,
  93

Bellhop, 15–17, 19
Bookkeeper, 69–73

Cashier, 58
Caterer, 7, 31, 51–55
Civil service exams, 84–85
Clerical work, 69–73
Computers, 9, 21, 22, 23, 27,
  30, 70
Contracts, 93–94
Convention planner, 13,
  63–67
Cruise director, 75–79

Discrimination, 93–94
Doorkeeper, 15, 18–19

Employment growth, 10

Food services, 13; see also
  Caterer; Truck-stop
  operator; Convention
  planner

Interviews, 89, 92

Language knowledge, 23, 27,
  39, 42
Letters of application, 85–88
Limousine driver, 33, 83

Motels, 17
Motorcoach driver, see Tour-
  bus driver
Museum guide, 42

Package deals, 12
Porter, 16
Preparation, 81–83

Résumé, 86

Seasonal work, 39
Secretary, 66, 69–73, 83, 87

Taxi dispatcher, 45–49, 83
Tour-bus driver, 33, 35–37
Tour guide, 30, 39–43, 83
Travel agent, 7, 9, 11, 21,
  27–31, 66, 83, 88
Truck-stop operator, 13,
  57–61